*Survive the corporate maze and achieve your dreams.*

# Woman ... You Rock!

A practical guide to Leverage strengths,
Build network, Negotiate smarter and
Live up to your true potential

To my parents for bringing up my sister and me for being at par.

To my husband, who has always supported me and been the role model for our two sons.

And my in-laws who have encouraged me to go on and live my dreams.

# Contents

Introduction ..................................................... ..........8

Chapter 1: Building the Base ...................................13

Chapter 2: Keep on moving....................................26

Chapter 3: Negotiating for more.................... .......34

Chapter 4: Network is your Net-worth ............_.......47

Chapter 5: Un-Politics...................................... ......58

Chapter 6: Trust That Gut ......................................65

Chapter 7: Family Matters......................................71

Chapter 8: Organize life: De-clutter stream-line.79

Chapter 9: Passion Projects............................_.....88

Chapter 10: Loving Yourself............................. ....96

Chapter 11: The final word....................................108

Acknowledgements................................................113

# Disclaimer

The objective of the book is to share learning from experiences. It reflects the author's present recollections of experiences over time. Names and characters have been changed, and some events have been compressed.

The advice and strategies found within may not be suitable for every situation. Reader discretion is advised to fit the suggestions to your context.

# Introduction

This book has been in my mind for a long time. I have gone through the words in my head over and over again. In an instant, as each word lights up the screen, it takes a life of its own.

This is the story of my transitioning from a naïve girl to a woman learning the ropes each day, bit by bit.

Women across the world are on a journey to achieve success on their terms. Things have been shifting fast all around. The pandemic year behind us has taught us a lot, and it has changed the dynamics of the business world and each home. With families, housebound 24/7, with no other social interaction, have got closer than ever. On the other extreme, it is like being confined to four walls, and some have fought like never before. The 'storming' is a stage in all sorts of team formation. The lockdown meant seeing each other every day, and it left not many options but to keep it cool or kiss and makeup.

The professional world saw a tremendous transition as well. From 'you need to be in the office at 9 am sharp!' to 'you need to work-from-home every day!' The changes were sharp and sudden. It was like being thrown at the deep end of the pool all of a sudden. The companies with sound IT systems could make the transition almost seamlessly. Others floundered a bit till they could adapt to the new normal.

How did this change-over impact women in the workforce? Women have been trying for a long-time to establish a work-life balance, only to be told that it was a myth and work-life integration may be a better deal! While trying that, it still left them wondering, 'Can I have it all?'. Then came the pandemic and wiped all myths around. Suddenly, the reality started biting. The chunk of household chores suddenly landed on the plate of the lady of the house. Whether working or not, the women found themselves attempting an unending list of tasks. With no household help, it was all about self-help!

Though it may have been a lopsided division of labour to start with, soon, the longevity of the lockdown started becoming clear. The families understood that they were in it for a long haul. The only way to tide through the situation was to try to work together.

Companies suddenly started realizing the benefits of remote working. The managers realised that even without their 'supervision', work was still getting done.

So, now the question remains, how do women make their way along the corporate echelons? Is this the new reality, and is a new world order emerging? How can women ace this new journey with panache?

The book covers all aspects that could potentially help in the journey.

Chapter 1 talks about building a solid base. About getting the proper education and professional credentials. Then the next step is about taking on this with the proper certifications. Throw in life skills like cooking and essential financial management, and you can set yourself up for success.

Chapter 2 covers the important bit about remaining agile and making the right career moves. This could be through internal role movements or taking up a new position in another organisation. The intent is to avoid stagnation and achieve faster growth.

Chapter 3 covers an essential skill of negotiation. Whether you need to negotiate a new job offer or negotiate for a raise at the existing organisation, this skill can be a game-changer. It covers aspects like highlighting the value you bring through your work and linking that to what you save or earn for the company.

Chapter 4 points out the significance of having a strong network of people you can trust and who can support you when needed. At times you may need to become your spokesperson and share with enthusiasm what you are working on. Sharing your achievements and working actively to create visibility for your projects is an essential part as well.

Chapter 5 talks about the tricky word 'Un-politics'. Where there are people, there would be a mix of agendas. Understanding people and what makes them tick is important to navigate your way up the ladder. Being genuinely interested in people and connecting with them both in-office and informal settings can help. Remain aware and leverage the knowledge of experienced colleagues to learn about the way things operate.

Chapter 6 is all about trusting your gut. Sometimes the 'gut feeling' is hard to explain and justify. You just continue to trust yourself and believe. The more you believe, the more you will be able to leverage this unique strength. What logic may not be able to provide can be complimented with these internal feelings.

Chapter 7 is all about your family. Your family plays a vital role in your success. The corporate journey has its ups and downs. Having a supportive family does ease the pressure a bit. Whether it is your parents, spouse, kids, or in-laws, enrolling them in your goals and achievements is a must.

Chapter 8 is about getting the household set-up organized. Designate a space and place for things and stick them in. Stream-line kitchen and grocery inventory processes to make them less dependent on people. It is imperative to have an unwavering backup system at home to put your best professional foot forward. This includes ensuring good child care for your kids. Only when kids are well taken care of, can you focus on your work goals.

Chapter 9 is about looking for passion projects. These projects make your heart go boom. This is the work that engages your heart, mind, and soul. The task leverages your strengths and provides the right level of challenge. When you are working on this project, you find such joy that the process itself becomes a pleasure. Engaging in more of such projects can be a sure recipe for success.

Chapter 10 is about loving yourself. The world is like a mirror; it reflects what we think and feel. If you love yourself, the chances are that love will get reflected. Have a self-care routine including eating well, keeping yourself hydrated, sleeping enough, and exercising. Pray and tap into the power of the universe to make all your dreams comes true. And finally, believe in yourself as I do – **Woman ... You Rock!**

In the following few pages, I share some things that can help make small tweaks in all of the above areas, making a significant impact. All names are fictitious to ensure privacy and confidentiality.

# Chapter 1: Building the Base

First, get the base right. How do you ensure that you get a good job and make a long-lasting successful career?

Build a strong base for yourself. Lay the foundation solid and steady. What do I mean by that? Simply get your educational qualifications in place. Does academic degree matter? Yes, as a first step, I believe it does. It is not just about getting good scores in school or college. Getting foundational knowledge is the crucial part. Once you have the basics done, building on top of it takes less effort.

Another part is, getting yourself used to hard work and discipline. I would always wonder, do we need all the subjects that are taught in school? What has dawned on me only later, is that it gives an overview of how things operate around us. As we start connecting with diverse people, we have conversations that can draw on our previous knowledge collected over the years.

Being observant with an eye for detail can hold you in good stead as well. Just by noticing what is happening around you, you can continue to learn a lot. Look at people and watch how they react to certain situations. Learning is never a destination. It is a life-long process!

Let's us take the example of Saroj. Saroj was just completing her graduation when her parents arranged for a meeting with a prospective groom. The guy was a good match, and the family was well placed. Everything fell in place, and within a month, parents arranged the marriage. Though Saroj had plans to study, this was something unexpected. With a bit of courage, she suggested that maybe she should pursue her Master's degree one day. Though the family was a bit conservative, she could convince her in-laws. Even as she was about to complete her degree, she discovered that she was pregnant. Once her kid was big enough, Saroj again resumed her education and earned a degree in teaching. With this, she was now qualified to apply for teaching jobs. Soon she started as a trainee teacher at a school nearby. She retired from the same school as vice principal at the end of a successful career. Others would often quote her example of studying after marriage and then successfully continuing in her career.

The critical question to ask is, what is your own personal and professional ambition?

When I was studying, I had a clear mindset about what I wanted: a Master's degree. It was non-negotiable to me. Both of my parents had Master's degrees, and my sister was studying to become a Medical doctor. So, it was like a bare minimum that I expected from myself. Though this may not be a guarantee for success, I thought it could be a start.

My own bachelor's degree was in Information Technology. With the IT boom and everything around moving to automation, this seemed like a great option. I did explore other diverse areas like Mass Communications and Hotel management. But the odds were definitely in favour of B.I.T. This was a four-year course introduced newly in Delhi University and considered at par with Engineering. So, after much debate and careful consideration, it was decided that this would be the course that I would pursue.

Though I was performing well and getting good scores, I felt a bit unsure. It was not that I could not be good at it. The question was - could I be the best at it? After about three years in the course, I came across a fascinating subject – 'Organisation Behaviour'. This suddenly opened a new perspective for me about the field of 'Human resource management.' I was drawn to that right from the start. Pretty much from that moment, I knew that I might move into the 'people' direction with my next degree.

Then came the thought of Masters in Business Administration. I started finding out more about it. Talking to people in my extended family, I tried to figure out how to crack CAT (Common

Admission Test). Preparing for the entrance test was the first step.

I enrolled myself in a class to prepare for the exam. I diligently went to all classes and started practising as soon as I reached home. Quick revision helped to condense and crystallize in my mind the learning. I gave the CAT and got a reasonably good score. However, it was not good enough for an IIM. It got me a call from IMI.

That became my next pitstop for two years. At the end of which, I came out with an MBA in Human Resources.

> Rajini was a diligent student throughout her school and college. She had plans to start working as soon as she completed her bachelor's degree. The first teaching job she got was with a school. The pay was not very high, and the distance from her house was too much. The daily commute soon became too cumbersome. As soon as her marriage completed the first month, she decided to quit the job. Starting out married life and the travel time was becoming too much to handle. She quit and got busy with setting up her domestic life. Was this enough? Mostly yes, though sometimes, she did wonder, 'what if I had studied more and then followed through my career'?

It was clear that I would like to complete my studies before I got married. Things did play out a bit differently, though. I got married after the first year of my MBA. Then for the two-month internship period, I moved to Mumbai and completed the internship with Tata Motors. This was the time that I could spend with my husband before returning to Delhi to complete the remaining one year. Was it easy? No way. It was super hard. I almost travelled every month to Mumbai to catch up with him. Then focusing on studies right after getting married was not so easy either. It was all about changing gears and adapting once again.

What helped at that time was working with my group of friends. Sitting alone in my hostel room, I would find my thoughts drifting. So, one way was to get my head in the 'here and now', by studying in a group. This, in a way, was great because this strengthened my friendship with this super cool bunch of friends. Slowly I started to hang out with them and not just study with them. When you are in good company, time seems to fly. In a jiffy, the second year was over, and it was time to start my career.

I moved to Mumbai, this time for good. I started with Tata Consultancy Services in their Learning & Development department. The induction was for two weeks, and we stayed at the Hotel Sea Princess on Juhu Tara road. The hotel was overlooking the sea, yet we were so busy during the days that it might have been just once we went to the beach! This batch had people from all over India, and it seemed like such a diverse group of people. It was an excellent start for all of us who were just out of college. The experience was awesome and created great memories to last a lifetime. Induction program – 'Pitstop' laid the foundation of my career. I learned early in life that excellence would be a key differentiator.

As I moved to different roles, I gained experience that further added to my knowledge. There were ups and downs for sure, but each down taught me a lot. I would often reach out for books when I felt stuck. As I learned more, I realised the importance of connecting with senior colleagues who could become my sponsors. These are individuals who can see the spark in you at an early stage. As they have more visibility and credibility in the organisation, they can provide you with advice.

They also have access to others in leadership and can support your career progression. Being more experienced, they can share past experiences that can be valuable source of knowledge and information.

> Shalini was an ambitious and energetic professional. When she joined the organisation, she was an individual performer. Very soon, she took on additional responsibilities and showed leadership qualities in all her projects. With her performance and potential, she

was promoted quickly to the managerial role. Some of the team members who were her peers now started reporting to her. Suddenly, she felt a shift in the level of cooperation and collaboration within the team. Things went southwards, and the performance of the group started to drop. She tried to talk to the team and work out possible solutions, but nothing worked. Shalini ultimately decided to move on.

As a last resort, she spoke to her ex-boss, who was now a mentor. As she shared her story, she felt a burden lift off her chest. Then came the wise words about making the transition smooth. She would need to re-adjust her style of communication. It would need to be a delicate balance of authority and approachability. Shalini started applying the advice of her mentor and very soon found the team performance improve.

Finding a coach can be a game-changer as well. What does a coach do? The coach helps you take a step back and analyze your patterns. We can be engrossed in work and lose sight of the big picture. With a coach, you can take a bird's eye view of the situation and make better decisions. How do you find a coach? Sometimes by luck, the coach may find you. Else, you need to keep an eye on people who have a helping attitude. The coaching relationship evolves over a long period of time. Have the patience to stay with that. When you find a person who you feel can coach you, have the courage to ask. Suppose the person agrees, great. If not, then keep looking on. There may also be instances when you connect with different individuals to seek advice. This may not be ongoing coaching. It just works well enough.

There have been multiple instances when I have felt stuck, wondering what to do. Just talking to some of these individuals has helped immensely. The key here is to have multiple people you can trust and go to when needed.

Learning from peers can be another valuable resource. At times we have got complementary strengths. It makes a lot of sense to share the learning that we have with others. Also, asking for support is a sign of maturity. If we can ask the right questions and be open to learning from others, it can aid our career growth. When stuck, I have reached out to people who may know better about the subject. Yes, asking for help is more complicated than helping someone else. It does take courage and is a hit on the ego!

What if the person refuses to help? What if I do not get the solution? What if everyone else comes to know that I did not see the solution first? So many thoughts can cloud your mind. The ultimate thing to keep in mind is, that you will never know if you do not ask. It is ok to appear foolish for one time rather than stay stupid forever.

Even as you build your professional expertise, there may be some life skills that you may wish to sharpen. Cooking can be one such skill that can be developed. Being able to cook a basic meal needs to be a bare minimum for all family members. This can be a big boon in case study, or travel takes you away from home. If you can make basic recipes, then staying on your own will be a lesser challenge. Depending on your interest level, you can pick on advanced skills like baking. Multiple learning avenues are present, like YouTube videos and finding online recipes. This can be just that factor that creates delight for family and friends as they experience your delectable recipes.

Another area worth having a focus on, is financial acumen. As you move to earn your money, managing finances get more critical. To be able to have your money invested in the right places can be essential for financial freedom. Good saving habits can help you to create a kitty for your retirement and all other significant milestones in between. You may either need to brush up on your knowledge or find a financial consultant who can be trusted.

Lastly, with many changes taking place around us, we need to keep updating ourselves on technology. There are apps available to help with day-to-day work. Being resourceful and trying out hacks to improve our productivity, is the way forward. If technology is something that you are afraid of, ask for help. Reverse mentoring by younger colleagues or by kids can help you pick these skills quickly. If there is a better and faster way of doing things, why not try it? Even if you fail the first time, what if you can save time every day going forward? Life requires us to keep learning and keep moving ahead. In the next chapter we will discuss how do we keep the momentum and keep moving ahead.

## **ASK YOURSELF:**

Do not underestimate the power of knowledge. Whatever your area of initial studies, keep trying to find your area of passion. Read more, learn more and keep working to hone your skills. Some questions to think about:

- Given your current education, would you like to specialise further by going ahead and adding another qualification?

- Has there been a subject area where you would like to go deeper? Is there a professional course/certification in the same area that you would like to pursue?

- Do you have friends with whom you can work to achieve your future aspirations?

- Do you reach out and ask for help when you are stuck or need help?

- Have you tried reaching out to your role models or someone you look up to for guidance?

- Are you taking some initial steps that can give you a head-start in your career?

- Are you consciously moving towards the area that will make you feel fulfilled?

## BUILD THE BASE

### Core
To get a job basic educational qualifications and foundational knowledge are required. Staying disciplined and putting in hard work also goes a long way in career growth.

### Reflect
Do you want to specialise in your current subject? Do you want to pursue a professional course? Do you reach out to seek help when stuck? Do you reach out to role models for guidance?

### Key Practices
Connect with senior colleagues who could be your sponsors

Find a coach or hope that the coach finds you!

Learn from peers they are a valuable resource

Ask for support when you are stuck that is a sign of maturity

### Explore
Life skills like cooking and managing finances

Learn technology from apps or young generation or even your kids!

### Potential Journeys
Get an education and keep on upskilling

Work hard and be disciplined

Become observant

Strive for excellence

Find a coach or a mentor

# Chapter 2: Keep on moving

What I am recommending is not just about changing jobs or hopping from company to company. The idea is to keep yourself growing. It could mean moving upward or side-ways within the same organisation. Check if the company encourages cross-functional moves or do they have a job rotation policy.

Especially in the initial years of the career, changing roles allows you to have an opportunity to apply knowledge in varied contexts. This will enable you to learn more and also know where your core strengths lie. You can then select the most suited vertical in which you would like to specialise.

Carol Dweck, in her Ted Talk, shares about the growth mindset. This growth mindset is based on the belief that your basic qualities can cultivate through your efforts. The passion for stretching yourself and sticking to it, even when it's not going well, is the hallmark of the growth mindset. This mindset allows people to thrive during some of the most challenging times in their lives. If we can develop a growth mindset, we will create a trajectory for lifetime growth.

You could start as a generalist and then move to a specialist track. In the initial years, it is ok to take some risks and try out possible options. Ascertain what works for you and what does not. It is a better proposition to figure out what you simply hate at the onset.

There was a lady who joined the corporate sector with me. Let us call her Radhika. She was selected to work in the same department as me. Initially, working on a project took her to a distant city for six months. Another stint then followed this in an aligned department. Having got an early exposure, she felt it was time for her to move. Completing two years in the organisation, she resigned and moved to a higher position in another company.

In my case, I started in the Learning & Development (L & D) track and then went on to a more generalist profile that has given me an excellent overall understanding. Though in my case, it was a bit reverse. Yet, for me, L & D always remains closest to my heart. So, in hindsight, that worked out fine.

There are no right or wrong options. It is just that quick movement prevents stagnation. Early in the career, getting in a comfort zone can lead to stunted growth. From a life stage perspective, being single with limited responsibilities gives you more freedom to explore and try out permutations and combinations. Location can be one of the variables you could try. Different industries and sectors could be another thing to explore.

I had met this woman, Veronica, who had about ten years of experience in her company. When the company decided to open a branch in London, she raised her hand. She became one of the members who helped put up the business there. The international exposure was a huge learning opportunity. It did mean though that she had to leave her five-year daughter in the care of her mother for those six months. The company could not afford to support the cost of the entire family moving at that point. Accepting some of the trade-offs is also part of the journey. Veronica did that, and that stint helped her build her profile and skill set.

Another thing that can help is, taking up professional courses and certifications along the way. Continuous ongoing learning is the way forward. With the fast-paced changes happening worldwide, the only way to survive or thrive is by acquiring new skills. The sounding board of your education is the primary school. It has got you here. To advance in your career and life, you need to keep upgrading. Even the best model of the phone needs to have upgrades periodically!

I have always been on the lookout for what more can I learn? TCS was a learning organisation that provided many avenues for learning. There were many formal learning options. There were libraries in the offices, and you could issue multiple books at any time. With my appetite for learning, it was almost like being in heaven.

On my initiative, I did a few courses as well. These were all things that pulled me. I would take up exciting things and then gave them my heart, mind, and soul. Counselling skills certification was one such thing. I had always felt a compelling pull towards human psychology. This course, I felt, would be a great way to channel my curiosity for the field. I loved the course and everything that we did in it. For the final assessment, I prepared well and got the best score across the entire batch.

Moving forward a couple of years, I was a part of the training on Human-Centered Design. It was all about innovation using Design Thinking tools. It was intriguing to know that the session could also be facilitated without being a subject matter expert. So, you leverage the strengths of the participants and yet create tangible outcomes.

Such courses make you future-ready. They add value to you as a professional, and you can then create an impact in any organisation you go to. If you are looking at starting your own business, varied education and experiences can come in handy.

> Kirti was a cooking coach at a professional catering institute. She went on to learn about food preservation and the art of pickling. With this additional qualification, she decided to follow her passion in a more profound and more fulfilling way. She started a venture, training women to make pickles, and started marketing for them. It helped these women to have a steady income. She began writing books and sharing her recipes widely. Kirti experimented with a YouTube channel and

soon had a huge follower base. Not only was she able to financially earn more, but she could help many women become financially independent. The decision to move her career in a different direction proved to be a turning point for her.

After nine years at TCS, I moved to the next organisation, Owens Corning. Were the nine years too long? Not really. This was also a time when I had both my kids. So, in a way, I did have those two breaks. So, the monotony never set in. When I returned from my maternity leave, I moved into new roles. The large size of the organisation provided for multiple role opportunities to move internally.

After nine years, I did feel I had exposure to all areas of HR, and it was time for moving on. With my learning appetite, I thought it would be good to try a different industry. Owens Corning was into the manufacturing sector and hence a very different experience from the IT sector. I stayed on for two years, where I could work across a lot of initiatives. The trick is to keep judging when it is time to move. Listen to your inner voice and make the transitions.

With time I have realised the significance of agility. To be able to move quickly and deftly in the direction of my life's purpose, one of the books that I often go back to is, 'Who Moved My Cheese?' A very profound concept of managing change has been put in a very simplistic way. I often tell myself that I need to keep my running shoes handy. I do not want to hang the boots on the wall and slip into a comfort zone.

As we gain more experience, the initial excitement of the job starts waning. The tasks start to become mundane. That is the time to explore what new could be done. Should you change the organisation or not? Do you have leaders that inspire you? Do you have peers that are more like friends? Do you sense that your values are aligned with the organisation? If yes, then continue, and try to look for suitable newer opportunities. You may need to raise your hand and negotiate for what you want. We may look at negotiation as a one-time activity before joining a company. That's not true—more about this in the next chapter. You need to negotiate your way to success each time you need additional resources or support.

## **ASK YOURSELF:**

The maximum growth happens just outside our comfort zone. Once you start getting too comfortable, you need to ask yourself:

- Are you curious enough to ask questions regularly?
- Do you have a growth mindset and believe that you can learn everything?
- Are you leveraging the new channels of learning?
- Do you feel that you have enough learning opportunities in your current workspace? Are these learning opportunities taking you to the next level of growth?
- Is lateral movement or finding another role internally possible?
- How to decide when to start looking for roles outside the organisation?
- In which direction do you want to steer your career with the next move?

## KEEP ON MOVING

### Core
Changing job roles gives an opportunity to apply knowledge in various contexts and find our strength areas which may be further developed. Listen to your inner voice and move!

### Reflect
Do you want to move from a generalist to a specialist role? Are your values aligned with your organisation? Do you have a growth mindset? Do you want to work in another industry?

### Key Practices
Check if your company has a job rotation policy

Cultivate a growth mindset and be willing to learn new skills for career growth

Take up professional courses and certifications to upskill

You are the best judge of when to move - listen to your inner voice as your guide

### Explore
Different locations, travel for work

Different sectors and industries

Courses that interest you

Professional certifications
Internal transfers

### Potential Journeys
Move to a new role when you think it is time

Generalist to a specialist role or vice versa

Look for opportunities to travel for work

Take professional courses

# Chapter 3: Negotiating for more

We want our work to speak and create the path ahead for us. In an ideal world, can this work – sure! Only the world is not perfect. Leaders significantly higher up the ladder have limited time. They may not have the visibility to the wonderful work you may be churning out until one of your immediate superiors is your advocate and works to share the impact you create.

So, in normal circumstances, you need to showcase your work and make it a point to create the visibility you feel you deserve.

Whether it is getting a raise at your current job or a better salary offer at a new job – remember it is a 'negotiation' as much as we would like our bosses to read our minds and pay us the money that we should get. It may not happen until you actively go about the conversation that highlights the value you create. More the numbers you can add, better the strength of the argument.

It could come from a space of humility, but, keeping low key does not help. You may think that you can keep sharing of your accomplishments for the year-end performance review. By then, it may be too late. Decisions are often taken ahead of time, not just during the review discussion—human beings rely on perception and the grapevine to form opinions. If there is a lack of information, the chances are that the available inputs from others may form the basis of your reviews.

This in a way is like handing over the controls of your future to others. However, well-intentioned, people have their agendas. You may not be on the priority list of all. It may make sense not to leave things to chance and actively manage your visibility and perception in the organisation.

When the time comes, you may need to present a lot of data and feedback that you would have collected over months. This can come in handy when you need to highlight your talent and achievements to multiple levels of managers.

There is a quote that I found so accurate.

### *'You don't get what you deserve. You get what you negotiate for!'*

As women, we are brought up with many nice thoughts about *karma* and about just putting your head down and working hard. The rewards of this hard work will follow automatically. I wish that were true at all times. Many experiences later and through a significant amount of unlearning, I discovered, this is not true in each small situation! The universe wants us to work to get a special reward. Overall in life, the 'law of karma' may apply. But then asking for what you rightfully deserve is your karma. Expecting God to descend for each appraisal discussion may be a bit too much to expect!

Another pitfall to avoid is the need for perfection! Sometimes we overthink and overanalyze in our quest for perfection. It is good to have deliverables that are meeting the standards. If we keep going back to the drawing board, then it might be good to question. Is this the need of the client or your manager, or your own need to overcorrect?

There are too many people doing hard work. And not to take away anything from anyone, they may be moderately successful too! How does that impact you? There are fewer positions as you move up in the organisation. For every subsequent upward or lateral move, you need to prove yourself. Add to it the unconscious bias that may be at play.

It is not hard to notice that for men, sharing their achievements comes easily. You may find that a normal conversation quickly shifts focus and starts sounding like a sales pitch. Imagine what happens when a male colleague gives these impromptu elevator pitches to a varied audience across the organisation. Firstly, it creates a positive buzz for him. Secondly, it creates a collective impression on a group of people, some of whom might be decision-makers, subsequently. Lastly, it provides additional information to the organisation about some of the things this person is working on.

Does it matter? You may ask!

I would love to say – Naah!

But, unfortunately, it does.

Randhir was a new hire who came from another IT firm. He was an extrovert and could easily talk to anyone. As he got familiar with the team, he started sharing stories about his past successful projects. Weeks turned to months, and he settled in the team and created a mark with his work. At the same time, he always made it a point to share the progress with his project leader. He kept his skip-level manager also informed of key initiatives that he was taking. Within the next two years, he was promoted and sent for an on-site opportunity the year after. It was a combination of hard work and the ability to show the case that opened his way to getting the right option.

Imagine the contrasting situation where a female employee who is actively working on multiple projects does not invest much time positioning her achievements. Instead, she does not want to take away precious time from her work to try and show how impactful her deliverables will be. She continues to work harder and harder, hoping that someone may notice and reward her with a good rating or an increment at the end of the year. Well, if nothing else, at least some positive words of encouragement or verbal praise!

In a linear causal effect cycle, this would happen. But, the organisational world is complicated and is getting more so. With multiple changes and dynamics evolving each day, the attention span of decision-makers is also limited.

When left to itself, the chances are that negative news will flow upwards rather quickly than any positive contributions – hypothetically, if there is any escalation or client complaint. What do you think will happen? The months of work that was happening smoothly will be forgotten. What would get discussed and highlighted would be the issues currently on the table.

That is when providing any explanation would sound defensive. And yes, you may feel defensive when months of good work is put on the back-burner and light is shone on that one error!

> Jyoti was working on a high-intensity project. The client had given a short timeline and was pressing the team to deliver at the earliest. It was almost like working round the clock. The first 3 phases of the project had been delivered, and the client was now waiting for the last deliverable. The project was going fine, and the project manager, Vijay, had not heard anything adverse.
>
> Given that Jyoti was a quiet worker, she hoped that things were ok. When the last phase was delivered, the client called Vijay

directly and mentioned how the final deliverable did not meet his expectation. The team called a meeting and decided how they would manage the situation. Jyoti was hugely disappointed with the turn of events. From a project that was going well to a client escalation, she felt lost and dejected.

Well, now let's just rewind. What could be done differently to avoid this situation?

Jyoti could have taken out some time to share the report for each deliverable. She could have taken the client's feedback after each phase and shared it with Vijay. Sharing this would have created positive precedence. Then the negative review would be like a stand-alone stray instance.

When things are going well – budget time – share the good news upwards. Do this often and proactively. You will thank yourself for doing so in the future.

If you feel that you are underpaid, what do you do? Quietly find another job and move? Or can you stay on and bring it to the awareness of others with facts? The first task is to collect the points. Do you have bench marking data of the industry? Have you got an idea of how people within your organisation are placed? Can you put these data pieces together to provide a business justification for your raise?

Research shows that women are often underpaid for delivering the same work as their male counterparts. This may be a systemic issue that needs to be fixed over a while. Though many organisations are trying to fix that, it may take longer to reach parity.

The other aspect is what value you bring to the organisation. Can you prove the money you are helping the organisation make or save in no uncertain terms? Every transaction is a give and take. If your contribution is high, the company may wish to retain you.

After careful evaluation, you need to bring these facts to the table and discuss them with your supervisor. It is often a good idea to practise the conversation well before your meeting. You may wish to add the financial commitments that you need to meet. And then share objectively the facts that you have collected about how your salary needs to be increased. This needs to be both from external market parity and internal pay equity perspective. Share your deliverables and specific initiatives that you have taken recently. State your expectations in clear monetary terms. The more homework that you have done, the better prepared you will appear in this conversation.

You may also wish to have this conversation with the other decision-makers, in the hierarchy. It may be wise to check what are the acceptable norms. Are you allowed to talk to your skip-level manager? Can you reach out to other stakeholders? Whom do you trust the most to support your case?

Negotiating for salary raise while you are working at the organisation may not seem easy. But it is worth it. It is also better than resigning and then re-negotiating as per the offer you have in hand. It also leaves the other organisation in a lurch.

When you do decide to switch, you would again need to negotiate your salary offer. The stereotype of 'girls are not good at Maths' plays in our minds at times. We need to get over the fear of numbers or coming across as greedy. Many of our values like 'manage your needs as per your means' have left us with mixed feelings towards money. Add to that the other ideas like 'hard-work is the best policy'. Women are often groomed to work and then not demand their share of the money. It is one of the ideas around 'being a good girl who is congenial and sweet'.

> Nishi was changing jobs after six years. She had been a consistent performer and had many projects to show her ability. After the three rounds of an interview, the new company was ready to make an offer. They asked Nishi for her expectation, and she mentioned 'as per market'. When the first offer came, it was 10% more than her current salary. Was Nishi disappointed? Yes, she was. She did not feel valued. In her current company, she had a good

network, and she liked her work. Suddenly, it made no sense for her to move. She declined the offer and continued in her current organisation. Her reason was that she did not want to negotiate!

As much as we need to negotiate hard outside, we need to re-define our internal self-talk. Address any value-based conflict internally before you negotiate. Else, you may run the risk of self-sabotage.

In case of a new job, when you are ready to accept the offer, ask the organisation for more details. What is the level that you are being placed at? What is the pay range for that level? Are you already towards the upper end of that pay range? How often do promotions happen? When can you expect your next increment? What is the average percentage of increment each year? These may seem like many questions, but you will realise the value once you join the new organisation.

When you are a new hire, you have no idea how the organisation's compensation policy works. Your best shot at knowing is to ask some questions before you sign on the dotted line. Asking for more than the initial offer is not a bad thing. Putting across your expectations is not bad either. There is no rule that you cannot ask for a 50% hike. The company may not meet it, but at least you will give them a chance to move as close as possible to your expectations. It is uncomfortable for women to put a figure when asked for their expectations. When it comes to men, the reply is almost instant, and they sound definite.

This is an area I have struggled with as well. It may well come from my childhood grooming and the idea of what fits within the 'good girl' image that I was taught to strive for. The idea is to keep trying till you get good at it.

Contrary to Nishi's case, Sunaina was working in a bank for almost four years. She was looking passively for a job change. When a head-hunter called her, she agreed to interview as the role sounded promising. She completed her interview rounds. Before making the offer, the new bank asked her expectation. Sunaina had done her research and was ready to share a detailed explanation of why she expected a 50% hike. Though the bank felt that it was quite a high expectation, they offered her a 30% jump. After multiple rounds of discussions, the bank gave her a final offer of 35%. She accepted and joined the bank a month later. As she became familiar with the compensation system, she realised that she had been placed well. Happy with her negotiation skills and starting at the right level, she went on to work at that bank for many years.

Negotiation skills are not just for sales' people. Each of us needs to negotiate our way to success. So, start learning more on this topic and then get comfortable doing it!

## **ASK YOURSELF:**

Negotiation is a skill to imbibe, whether it is for a salary offer at a new organisation or an increment or promotion at your current workplace. Evaluate for yourself:

- Do I feel valued enough in the organisation intellectually as well as financially?

- Is my current salary at par with the current market level for my experience?

- Am I internally placed at an equitable salary and grade to comparable peers?

- Do I spend time regularly collecting data and evidence to support my impact on the organisation's success?

- Am I clear about my expected salary and the percentage hike that I want?

- Have you thought-through and are clear about the definite non-negotiables?

- Have I negotiated the offer being made by the new organisation?

# NEGOTIATING FOR MORE

## Core
Make your work visible to your superiors in order to negotiate a high earning. Be open to ask for what you want to earn. Learn the art of negotiation in current job or a new job

## Reflect
Do you feel valued at your current organisation? Are you clear about your expectations of the upcoming hike in salary? Are you paid equitably as compared to your peers?

## Key Practices
Make your immediate superior your advocate about your work

Use numbers as much as possible to negotiate a better expected salary that you want

Don't wait until year end to discuss about your performance as opinions are formed much in advance. Share continuously

Don't fall in the trap of being a good girl and don't feel guilty about making money you deserve

## Explore
If underpaid, collect facts about your salary, show what value you bring and be clear in monetary terms of what you want to earn; negotiate by asking questions before accepting a job

## Potential Journeys
Become comfortable to share about your work around the year and don't feel guilty asking for more money; understand there is unconscious bias that maybe at play against you

# Chapter 4: Network is your Net-worth

Girls are often brought up believing that fairness is a given. Multiple ideas of fairness are continually fed in. 'Do good and get good'. 'Goodness begets goodness'.

All these are great ideas, to begin with. They are even almost perfect. Only that the reality is far from perfect. When we move into the real world, suddenly, we find ourselves at a loss. The truth dawns that the concepts that were continuously fed into the brain may not be a hundred per cent true!

There is then a need to re-evaluate the voice in the head. It could be your mom telling you that life is all about making adjustments. Or your dad's voice telling you to do your best and leave the rest.

Hard work and efforts are necessary for life. I would say that it is the base or foundation on which you can build the tower of your credentials. Is that enough? I would say 'hell no!'

In any organisation, the performance management system attempts to measure performance. Yet, it is based on the premise that everything is measurable. Conceptually, this makes for an objective and robust performance management tool. In reality, not everything can be quantified neatly into data. Many factors cannot be measured, and in those cases, managers fall back on informal measures. These could be feedback from peers or cross-functional superiors. In those situations, perception becomes a critical piece of the jigsaw puzzle.

You may be putting in 16 or 18 hours each day, yet one negative feedback could ruin your chances of that coveted promotion. Whereas if you have been networking well and managing your buzz in the organisation proactively, positive feedback can hugely turn the tide in your favour.

For most women, there is this initial resistance to networking. Multiple thoughts could surface up when you think about networking. 'Why should I bother? I am working so hard anyway! I would much rather my work speak for me. I do not want to suck up to anyone. I don't want to come across as a social climber!'

These come from conditioning where girls are brought up to interact with a small circle of close friends. Be safe rather than sorry. Not to talk to strangers. Not to step out after sun-down. Well-intended parents want to keep their daughters safe within the confines of a close group of known people. This is great when we have a linear path to tread. While you are in school, you have only your grades to worry about, this approach is just fine.

Yet, in a corporate environment, you are now working in a cross-gender team. Opportunities are limited, and competition is cut-throat. When pitted against men, women find the habit of not networking, reducing their chances of winning substantially.

Boys are brought up with a smaller list of 'to do' and 'not to do'. The restrictions are less, and they are allowed to mingle around freely. Sometimes they fall and learn the hard way. Whether it is stepping out of the house or playing with strangers, the warnings are much less.

This gives boys a head start in dealing with people and coping with varied networking scenarios. As they grow up and enter the organisations, they quickly form the boys club. They can continue to spend after-work hours catching up on a beer. Women continue to rush home to carry on with the home duties and prefer to skip anything 'not directly considered work'.

It took me some time to realise my patterns. I was doing what I did during my childhood – to do what was told. Only now, I was a grown-up woman! I was now able to ensure my safety and use these opportunities to connect with people informally.

What is the big deal – you may wonder! We can catch up over lunch or a coffee during office hours. Yes and no! Sometimes the environment is everything. The kind of ice-breaking that can happen over a drink cannot occur after gulping many coffees in the office pantry.

People need to feel comfortable before they open up to you. They need to trust you and like you enough to be able to confide in you. Trust develops slowly and can be built over some time. During work parties, people often let their guard down. They can let go of their work masks. The discussion that can be a high-risk conversation in the office can become an after-drink banter. This can help you to exchange the content without the fear of judgment

And, I am not talking about getting soddenly drunk and letting go. It is just about picking up a drink to allow conversations to flow and allowing the ambience to keep the stakes low. As I started interacting with colleagues during off-sites over dinner and drinks, I realised the importance of informal networking.

Another great way to create a cross-location network is travel. Whether it is within the country or international, work-related travel provides a unique opportunity to form ties with people you do not meet daily. Face-to-face meetings can work wonders to develop quick connections. Not only you can know the people. You also allow them to learn more about you. It is essential in these meetings to prepare well and unambiguously state your strength areas.

As women, we are taught not to ruffle too many feathers. We are reminded to 'go with the flow.' Sometimes it is essential to articulate what we stand for clearly. This has been an edge that I have been working on consciously. When we do not state what our perspective is, we leave ourselves open to interpretation. This perception may be often far from reality.

In the lack of information, the decisions could move either way – in our favour or against us. The only way to influence decisions is by proactively sharing information about what you are doing.

A lot of male colleagues become their spokesperson and go on to share with enthusiasm what they are working on. While women employees tend to keep it low-key.

To add to the story of Sharon, she learned the hard way. After the performance rating fiasco, she started opening up to colleagues.

***Desperate situations call for desperate measures.***

According to Brené Brown, vulnerability can create. When we share our stories of defeat and expose the real emotions within, people can empathize. In those moments, Sharon felt a sinking feeling. And she was looking for any support to help her from drowning. As she confided more in the trust-worthy people around her, she saw strong bonds forming instantly. These bonds opened space for relations to grow and get strengthened. Precisely this was what she should have done initially. Being naïve and slightly less politically inclined, she had ignored this.

Now with a vengeance, she took to working on every task diligently and creating a trail of successful wins. She plugged whatever gaps that were picked on by her boss and started making her deliverables more visible. This not just made her feel confident but created a buzz of her performance and pace of delivering high-quality work.

Earlier, she had proceeded with caution and care not to offend anyone. Now she was performing with carefree abandon and was in the flow. The hours multiplied as she worked on back-to-back assignments, all lined up neatly. There was no doubt about her performance.

She was at the same time looking for options and interviewing for a role that would provide her space to grow. Soon enough, she got an offer that she found would be a good fit. She promptly accepted the same. She resigned from the organisation. The manager asked with a smile if she had made up her mind! She had made up her mind. It was a well-thought-through and intentional decision!

What Sharon learned the hard way was that 'networking' is not an option. It is the only way to survive in the corporate maze! Without a network, you may find yourself on a sticky wicket. It is like performing acrobatics mid-air without a safety net below. One freak fall, and you could find yourself badly hurt.

A little bit of awareness and a bit of effort early on might have changed the way Sharon's story played out.

There is another contrasting story of a woman, let's call her Ritika. She entered the organisation with her usual energy and zeal. She started performing well and soon created a positive vibe around her. She loved her work and went about it meticulously. A couple of months into the job, and things started shifting a bit. From the initial appreciation, there were now more questions. Questions around the value she was adding, what she was contributing, and so on.

It seemed as if the bubble had burst, and suddenly, she was encountering a different reality. She was just as surprised as was Sharon.

What had gone wrong? What was it that she needed to do more? She was still performing, then what was the issue?

Only in this case, Ritika knew that she had to do something.

She started listening to feedback more closely. She started confiding in team members and sharing what she was going through. She reached out to her friends to talk about her pain. Most importantly, she began taking steps to tide over the adverse environment. She kept delivering on her work deliverables. Anyways, that was not the problem. The gap was perceived in the visibility. To create her visibility, she began to share some of the work that she was doing.

Ritika had chosen to keep a low profile till that time. She knew that now she would need to reach out to individuals to build her safety net actively. It was evident that some would support her. On the other hand, few others did see others nothing to hide their despise.

The first step was to be able to distinguish between the two extremes. She had to figure out who she could trust. She could then work closely with this inner group to check what further steps she could take.

In one of the team meetings, she met an external consultant. The conversation was valuable, and she asked if he could coach her. This started another journey of self-discovery. Having a sounding board helped Ritika immensely. Also, now she could talk about things that were bothering her. Rather than remaining stuck in issues, she could speak through them.

Weeks rolled into months, and she continued to grow her network within the organisation. Talking to a colleague who had been in the organisation for a long time, made her understand the unsaid rules. She could see clearly what was needed and what she could do differently. On the other hand, she also started reaching out to those who may not always be on her side. This she did, not to win over the enemy, but, just to keep them close enough. She started speaking her mind more often. Part of creating your brand is all about talking about your innate strengths and working openly. The more she shared, the more this attracted appreciation.

People started noticing the difference in her approach. From a victim, she started feeling more in control. Did the work get any easy? No. Did she stop facing challenges? No.

It was just that Ritika was now more capable of facing those challenges than ever before. Which takes us to another important aspect that may evoke some discomfort. Hence, using the word 'un-politics' instead of 'politics'!

## **ASK YOURSELF:**

The question is not whether to network or not. The question is more about and when to network. Some ideas to start thinking about:

- Do you currently have a network within the organisation?
- Can you reach out to more individuals to widen your social circle?
- Do you have connections with people in the industry outside your organisation?
- Who are the people you can reach out to for support in times of crisis?
- Can you allocate some time each day to catch up with acquaintances?

# NETWORK IS YOUR NET WORTH

## Core

If you network and connect well and manage your buzz in the organisation proactively, positive feedback can hugely turn the tide in your favour.

The best way to influence decisions is by proactively sharing information about what you are doing.

## Reflect

Is your initial resistance to networking a function of your conditioning?

Are you visible enough along with being diligent?

Are you slowly building you brand?

Are you proactively building your case and regularly speaking about the impact?

## Key Practices

Get aware of your patterns and consciously work on your resistance to network.

Make the most of the informal networking opportunities by letting the work masks go.

Create a cross-location network by travelling within the country or

Leverage face to face meetings to develop quick connections. Not only you can know the people, allow them to learn more about you.

Prepare well for the meetings and unambiguously state your strengths areas and impact made.

| | |
|---|---|
| international, as it provides a unique opportunity to form ties. | Articulate what you stand for clearly and share with enthusiasm what you are working on. |

| **Explore** | **Potential Journeys** |
|---|---|
| Figuring out who you can trust | Give and take – Adam Grant |
| Having a sounding board to think aloud. | Continuing to grow your network within the organisation and outside. |
| Speaking through the issues rather than remaining stuck. | Seeing clearly what is needed and what can be done differently. |
| Speaking your mind more often | |

# Chapter 5: Un-Politics

Women often have mixed feelings about organisational politics. You may hate it, you may not like it, but you cannot deny it. Wherever there are individuals, there may be diversity in interests. At times the interests may be so divergent that it could lead to conflict.

Whether you term this as organisation politics or self-interest – it does not matter much. The truth is that you would need resources for achieving your goals and facilitating the same for your team. If you are unaware of the organisation dynamics and undercurrents, you may end up getting starved for necessary approvals and resources.

Experience is vital for individuals and the organisation. On the other hand, with the fast pace of change, it is doubtful that based on past experience alone, any individual can survive. What is needed is continuous development. Having a growth mindset helps in such cases. Where you keep learning and expanding your knowledge, not for any external gain but your betterment.

When individuals bow out of this learning process, their thought process starts stagnating. This is not to discount the multitude of ways in which individuals can learn. It can be through their people connect and by talking to peers or industry leaders. The bottom-line is to come up with innovation in their areas, to keep acing their game. If this does not happen, the result is a highly paid manager with a high level of insecurity. When the person feels insecure within, the chances are that they will try to find security outside.

**What we do not have within, we seek outside.**

These managers then need to make their position secure. For that, they will be ok to sacrifice any lower rung employee who may have a potential to threaten their position. In that case, what is your best option?

How do you secure your position? How do you ensure that you don't fall flat on your face when the carpet is pulled from under your feet? There will be those situations when the blame game starts, and you find yourself in the eye of the storm.

> There was this lady, let's call her Mona. She was going about doing her work and working through the highly complex matrix organisation structure. As she travelled to the various city offices, delivering her work, she felt that she was working round the clock. She was preparing for one assignment while on the plane, delivering the second while planning for the third. After one such trip,

she got a call from a colleague. He asked if everything was ok with her. She wondered why the question. The colleague explained that the boss had called after she left to check if the assignment was delivered well. Or rather to check if it had not gone so well! This seemed odd to this team member, and hence, he had called to check.

Mona felt an odd sense of doom come over her. She knew this manager did not like her. But this was weird and somewhat unbelievable. She did not know what to do or whom to talk to about this. Being new in the company, she did not have too many friends who were close enough. She got busy with her work and put that odd phone call behind her. She thought with all the high-visibility projects she was delivering, things will be ok.

The year-end came, and she was scheduled for the performance appraisal discussion. She saw one team member after the other go in ahead of her. Hers was the last discussion, and it was almost evening. She went in and sat down. The discussion was short, and she could not remember most of it. The only thing that she could understand was that somehow her rating was 'below average! Shock, dismay, shame, sadness seemed to envelope her. She felt like there was a huge rock placed on her heart. Somehow, she managed to pick her stuff and leave the office that day.

What was the learning for Mona?

She had chosen to ignore the writing on the wall! Believing that everything would be ok, she was behaving like an ostrich trying to bury its head in sand and imagining that the enemy would not be able to see or attack.

Big mistake! Big! Huge!

If someone in the power corridors does not like you. Rather let's say, actively dislikes you. They may try to create situations that could lead to your early exit.

What do you do?

You need to read the signs early. The sooner, the better. If you capture the early signs, however ugly they may be, you can defend yourself against a potential attack. The stronger you perform, there are chances of attracting attention, both negative and positive.

That is not to say that all people are bad. There will be people who would become your cheerleaders as you achieve one milestone after another. But there would be those who will get insecure. Then there would be those who will get jealous. They may try to pull you down in covert ways.

Remain alert and watchful. Connect with more experienced members to understand the context and complexities. Learn about the history of the organisation and its leaders. Be genuinely interested in people and connect with them both in-office and informal settings. Look out for people who come across as trustworthy. These will be the people whom you will need when you find yourself in the hot seat. Another thing to add here, is always trust your gut feelings. If something does not feel right, maybe it is not right! More about that in the next chapter.

Mona failed to do all of this. She started looking out and found another job in a few months.

## **ASK YOURSELF:**

We have been taught that 'politics' is a bad word. Hence, the title of this chapter is 'un-politics'! Call it what you like, but, do not ignore it. Try to introspect if 'politics' was just like another skill, would you still not want to learn it? What if your job depended on this skill? Would you still ignore it? We do not need to become a master of politics, and it is just about knowing enough to navigate our way. Ask questions like:

- Do you sense politics at play in your organisation?
- Are you aware of the grapevine and informal channels of communication?
- Do you have a circle of trusted team members who will support you if needed?
- Can you take a few steps to know more about people and what motivates them?
- What can you do to make your work visible and leave a lasting impression?

## UN-POLITICS

| Core | Reflect |
|---|---|
| Wherever there are individuals, there is politics as there may be diversity in interests. At times the interests may be so divergent that it could lead to conflict.<br><br>Having a growth mindset and always trusting your gut feelings helps. | If 'politics' was just like another skill, would you still not want to learn it?<br><br>The stronger you perform, there are chances of attracting attention, both negative and positive.<br><br>Life is not always fair. How about being fairly ready |

| Key Practices | |
|---|---|
| Keep learning and expanding your knowledge, not for any external gain but your betterment.<br><br>The bottom-line is to come up with innovation in your area to keep acing the game.<br><br>Read the writing on the wall early. The sooner, | If you capture the early signs, however ugly they may be, you can defend yourself against a potential attack.<br><br>Remain alert and watchful. Connect with more experienced members to understand the context and complexities. |

| | |
|---|---|
| the better | Be genuinely interested in people and connect with them in-office and informal settings. |

| **Explore** | **Potential Journeys** |
|---|---|
| Learning about the history of the organization and background of its leaders.<br><br>Looking out for people who come across as trustworthy.<br><br>Knowing enough politics to navigate your way | Survival of the Savvy - Rick Brandon and Merty Seldman<br><br>Nice Girls still don't get the corner office - Lois P. Frankel<br><br>Believing and chasing your own dreams |

## Chapter 6: Trust That Gut

You may have heard about using your intuition or gut feel while making decisions. Should we go as per gut, or should we base decisions on hard facts? You may ask the question, 'do I really have a strong intuition'?

We all have intuition. Simple! What we need to do is keep strengthening it. Just like any other skill, if you don't use it, you lose it. Conversely, the more we use it, the more we strengthen it.

How do we explain the gut feel? It is that feeling that you get from within, whenever you are deciding something important for you. It may feel like an inconsequential matter, but for you, it may be of some significance.

One of the ways to work with intuition is meditation. Just sitting quietly, all by yourself, with your eyes closed. That is when we allow ourselves to connect with our inner being. When the external noises subside, the inner voice can emerge. In the world today, we are drowning in an information overload. There is social media that is trying to influence us. We are being bombarded with information every minute. What's with the messages downloading into our phones each minute? It is almost as if you 'blink and you miss' situation.

It is essential to set aside time for quiet thinking and reflection. This gives the mind a chance to synthesize the information and condense all the data.

Whenever you are making decisions, find all the facts that you need to. Consult all the experts and your family if you need to. Get all the outside information sources vetted. Then decide to stop searching outside and dive within. The inner guidance is always helping us to get more aligned with our life purpose. The more we follow this inner voice, the more it becomes powerful and loud. If we ignore this voice, it gets feebler each time. Till the time we cease to hear and lose it completely.

I have always felt that I have strong intuitive power. And time and again, I have wondered about it. At a certain point in time, I may think, why am I getting this signal, and then the answer comes much later.

There have been some decisions that I made basis my intuition. When I was getting ready to do my Master's degree, I had decided to give the entrance test CAT again and attempt to get a better score. It would enable me to get into premiere management institutes like IIMs, which was my thought process. So, I got a call from another management institute, but I did not take admission until that time. Then my family and I went on a spiritual trip to an *aashram* in the Himalayas.

We spent about a week there. It seemed like a coincidence that another girl there had just got admitted to the same college. I just wondered if this was a sign from the universe. When I returned to Delhi, I thought maybe I need to investigate this sign. Re-evaluating my decision of dropping the year, I decided to try for admission from the same college. I went to meet the Dean of the college and attempt at getting admission. With some amount of persuasion, I was able to obtain permission to complete the admission process. That was it. Two years later, I was an MBA, passing out of the same college IMI.

In hindsight, was this the best decision? I think so. For me, it turned out well. I had a good level of learning and made some great friends. What I was most happy about was that I could complete my Master's degree. For me, that was the level of education that I wanted for myself, if not more!

Another area where I feel I have a good gut instinct is related to people. In most situations I think, I can understand the people and their inner motivations. These feelings have been proven correct multiple times. That has further strengthened my belief in this strength.

At times I have doubted my gut instinct that did not seem to have any apparent reason. Then, I have got the evidence later. And I have gone like, yeah, that is something that I was thinking anyways!

Often you make decisions based on the facts as presented on the profile. But your gut feeling points in another direction. There was one individual who lied about how he got my mobile number. There was another one who would speak in a charming and friendly manner. Both cases appeared very promising on paper. But people are not just about skills or qualifications. They are also their values and the way they relate with others. Those were the areas where they could not match up and eventually had to leave.

Sometimes these 'feelings' are hard to explain and justify. In those cases, you need to wait for evidence to surface. In other cases, just continue to trust yourself and believe. The more you believe, the more you will be able to leverage this unique strength.

Finding a life partner could be a decision that you might need to base on gut-instinct in addition to fact-finding. More on this and family in the next chapter.

## **ASK YOURSELF:**

Intuition can be a skill to leverage upon. You just need to tune in and follow the gut instinct. The more you use it, the stronger it gets. You can reflect on:

- Do I get a strong inner voice when I am trying to make a decision?
- Am I able to trust the inner voice and use that as an input to finalize my choices?
- Do I get a strong vibe about certain individuals?
- Can I use the gut instinct when I need to decide the basis of selective information?
- Has the 'gut instinct' proved to be the right option in the long run?

## TRUST THAT GUT

| Core | Reflect |
|---|---|
| The gut feel is that feeling that you get from within, whenever you are deciding something important for you.<br><br>The inner guidance is always helping us to get more aligned with our life purpose | Are we drowning in an information overload?<br><br>Often you make decisions based on the facts as presented. But if your gut feeling points in another direction how to proceed?<br><br>Is there an apparent reason to doubt your gut feel? |

## Key Practices

| | |
|---|---|
| One of the ways to work with intuition is meditation. When the external noises subside, the inner voice can emerge.<br><br>Set aside time for quiet thinking and reflection to allow inner guidance.<br><br>Follow the inner voice more and more to make it more powerful and loud | Whenever you are making decisions, find all the facts that you need to. Consult all the experts and your family if you need to. Get all the outside information sources vetted. Then decide to stop searching outside and dive within to check what feels appropriate or right in that situation |

| Explore | Potential Journeys |
|---|---|
| Going with your gut feel while analysing and choosing people.<br><br>Continuing to trust your instincts to leverage the unique strength of intuition.<br><br>Choosing gut feel over facts and evidence. | The power of intuition - Diane Brandon<br><br>Gut Feelings: The Intelligence of the Unconscious - Gerd Gigerenzer<br><br>Listening & honouring the inner voice every time<br><br>Taking decision inspite of reason, fact & evidence |

# Chapter 7: Family Matters

Pay close attention to this one key aspect - family. Your family plays an important role in your success. What you will hold important and how you will navigate your life depends on your family values. Most of these are passed on at a subconscious level as we are growing up. Family background and what your parents believed in, does play an important role.

We cannot change the belief system of our parents, but we can start becoming aware of our patterns. Once we are aware of our habits and practices, we can begin to change them.

While we cannot change the family we are born into, we can influence the decision about the family we marry into. It would be best to have a clear idea of some of the qualities you are looking for in your life partner. It may make sense to work with a friend through this exercise. Preferably someone who is married and knows the expectations that the relationship comes with. It will be essential for your partner to believe in your work and profession, for you to feel supported.

The jobs are no longer 9 to 5 vocations that you complete and then focus on home. The work requires all-engrossing attention that often spills over beyond official working hours. If you feel embarrassed about having to work hard, it will adversely impact your performance both at work and home. You will resent that you are trying to meet two opposite ends meet and feel like a failure.

So how do you ensure that you find a supportive life partner?

Ask questions, lots of them, first to yourself and then to your prospective life partner.

What is your idea of an ideal life partner? Do you want to have kids? When and how many? Do you know how to cook? Are you a morning person or a later night owl? Are you an introvert, or do you like to party often? What are your career goals? Do you prefer saving, or do you spend your salary on the first day it is credited? What are your family's expectations from your life partner? Would you be able to support each other in managing those expectations?

And then the most crucial question – what temperature do you set for the air conditioner at night? Just kidding! But then, this is a point for multiple battles in many homes.

***Charity begins at home.*** Always.

You need to understand yourself first. You can then attempt to understand another individual, once you are clear on your own life goals. You can then try to match them to see if there is alignment with the significant other.

When I got married, I was 22 years old and still developing my ideas around life and my goals.

Yet, I did check for some amount of thought alignment on important matters like my career life, like the freedom to make decisions, spend money in areas that I wanted to, or have a routine that I could set for myself.

As luck would have it, my husband is an early morning person, and I am a night owl. There are some things that you will discover later. Most couples find themselves having bang-opposite preferences for some of the items. That is unavoidable. You are looking for a partner, not a clone! You will have to accept those differences, and the sooner, the better! It is an idea that life provides you with a partner who has complementary strengths—leverage on the differences rather than fight over them. So being a late-night person, I mostly turn out the lights at night and put kids to bed. Being a morning person, my husband wakes up the kids and picks on the morning chores.

Coming to the next significant question - When do you have kids? Is there a right time? Is early better than later? Career first or kids first? One is better or two? Should you space them well or have them close together? Are twins the best? Is surrogacy a possibility? Is adoption an option?

There are no correct answers. As what you choose will depend on your unique situation. Your family may have some fixed beliefs. It will be up to you to either convince them or get convinced.

I had my first child when I was 24 years old. It was about two years into my career. The maternity break came at a time when I had sufficient time in that one role. When I resumed work, I moved into a different position. The second baby came when I was just around 30 years. From a biological clock perspective, this seemed like perfect timing. I did need that space between the two. I wanted my first child to be sufficiently independent before the next came along. Was I always sure about having two kids? Not really. There are some answers that you discover along the way.

Am I happy that we have two kids? Yes, absolutely.

During the lockdown, suddenly, the family unit became all-important.

Did I thank my stars that we had two kids? Most definitely, yes! They could manage pretty much everything in the house. Playing games, studying together and shared gadget time too! And, also helping in household chores.

Enrol your in-laws in your journey. It is important to have family support as you move along your career journey. It is not a straight path. There will be ups and downs. Making the family members walk alongside takes trust and courage. The more you share openly about both wins and losses, the closer you can partner together. When you are going through rough patches, sharing openly creates empathy. When you return home tired, you will need strong arms to support you. When you feel defeated, nothing works better than someone telling you 'it will be ok'.

My parents were always supportive of my work. As I moved along and gained more experience, I realised the importance of having my spouse's parents support as well.

Success is much sweeter when it is shared. You can savour the fruits of the hard work when you share them with family.

As I see my kids growing up, I find them inspirational. They have become the best cheerleaders for me to go on. Are there days when I feel my mother's guilt surfacing with multiple doubts? Yes, there are. Am I spending enough time with the kids? Do they think that their mom is not available? Am I a good mom?

When I asked my elder son one day, 'do you wish I were a stay-at-home mom?' He said, 'you are perfect the way you are.' The directness of his response touched me. And it did relieve me of some of the doubts. He then added cheekily, 'You are so much cool' compared to some of the other moms!

If I look back, it has been quite a ride. Having a supportive family does ease the pressure a bit. I have also seen women struggle to settle at a new job and manage everything back home. It may be more complex for some, and giving up may seem like an easier option. That is where some amount of planning and thinking ahead may help. It is a learning process, and I am still at it.

As a couple, we have a better understanding now. I see my husband taking an active interest in trying out new recipes. With his support, I am finding more time to focus on some of my projects. My elder son has started learning how to cook and can make chapatis. The younger one is taking the lead in some of the chores as well.

We are taking baby steps toward becoming a more collaborative household. The next step is to make this household more organized as shown in the next chapter.

## ASK YOURSELF:

The family will be an important element in your success. The way you leverage this as a strength rather than making it look like weakness is up to you. There are ways to weave in the various aspects:

- Is your family aligned with your professional and personal goals?
- Have your parents encouraged you to follow your professional dreams?
- Does your life partner support your career ambition and help with household chores?
- Are your in-laws comfortable with a working woman as their daughter-in-law?
- Are you grooming your kids to be independent and support in the household chores?

## FAMILY MATTERS

| **Core** | **Reflect** |
|---|---|
| Family plays an important role in your success. | What are your life goals and how do you want to approach them? |
| What you consider important and how you navigate your life depends on your family values. | How do you integrate work and life?<br><br>How to ensure a supportive life partner? |
| Making the family members walk alongside takes trust and courage. | When do you have kids?<br><br>Should you space them well or have them close together? |

| **Key Practices** | |
|---|---|
| Have a clear idea of the qualities you are looking for in your life partner.<br><br>Ask questions, lots of them, first to yourself and then to your prospective life partner<br><br>Check for some amount of thought alignment on important life matters | Accept difference in preferences of your life partner, and the sooner, the better! Leverage on the differences rather than fight over them<br><br>Build family synergy as you move along your career journey by enrolling your in-laws and kids. Openly deliberate to either convince them or get convinced. |

| **Explore** | **Potential Journeys** |
|---|---|
| Becoming aware of your inherent patterns | Women's Work - Zoe Young |
| Influencing the family, you marry into. | Happy Relationships at Home, Work & Play – Lucy Beresford |
| Sharing openly when going through a rough patch. | Encouraging every voice in a family |
| Shaping your kids as your best cheerleaders. | Building independence and self-sufficiency in kids |
| Becoming a more collaborative household. | |

# Chapter 8: Organize life: De-clutter stream-line

Organize the house and everything within it well. Designate a space and place for things and stick them in. Labelling and sorting out space shelves can be a great idea. What is typically called 5S!

Imagine a scenario when you have to travel for some work or an emergency. Can anyone else step in to manage your house while you are away for two days? How easy would it be for them to find their way around the kitchen? Would they be able to trace your groceries and other supplies in your pantry? Will they be calling you multiple times to ask, or will they be sorted?

Now incrementally, start working out your spaces to ensure that anyone at one glance can find things. The one-time initial exercise might take a bit longer. However, the subsequent revisits will be more of maintenance and require a shorter duration.

Another important aspect is to de-clutter. Yes, it is needed. Even though you may feel that you just don't buy anything! And you may have just thrown a whole lot of stuff! We need to de-clutter regularly. Period. Now, this could be monthly for some areas like the kitchen and pantry. But, for wardrobes and other cupboards, at least a quarterly de-clutter is required.

You may need to identify the go-to people to give away stuff that you no longer need. For example, if there is a charity or an NGO, you could consider giving away things to them. Else, find people nearby who can accept the hand-me-downs as appropriate.

Streamline processes to make them less dependent on people. For example, can your house run if you or your spouse is not on the scene for a day? Can it run smoothly if the maid or nanny calls in sick in the morning?

You may not be able to achieve 100% people-independent processes but have back-ups in place. For example, can the nanny support the cooking for a bit? Can the maid serve the kids' lunch if needed? Having a staff to run the home is excellent. But, is one person able to substitute for another, in case needed?

You need to invest in people. Simple. When you have workers, allow them to work peacefully, and the people will integrate slowly with your life. You can then trust them and let them do their work! While you go and achieve magic in your workspace!

Another thing to check is how strong your support network is? Do you have friendly neighbours ready to help? It is said that the next-door neighbour is sometimes closer than your closest kin. So in the time of need or emergency, it may be the doorbell on the door next to you that you might need to ring.

We had an elderly couple living on our floor. One day the old gentlemen suddenly rang the bell. Their daughter had fainted and needed a doctor. We rushed over to their assistance and called on a doctor living in the building. The doctor gave some quick first-aid till she felt better. Then suggested we take her to the hospital till her husband arrives. This incident made me realise how important it is to have someone next door quickly provide support when needed.

It is a great help to have friendly neighbours, especially if you have small kids. The advantage is that the kids have a go-to place when they feel like it. This gives working mothers a breathing space.

> Sangeeta was an independent consultant, with her work requiring a lot of travel. She had a small daughter Tia who was around six years old. She would often go over to the house next door for a couple of hours each day after school. There she felt cared for and welcomed. She was a little bundle of energy that the family next door loved to have over. So while her mother was away, this relation in a way, fulfilled her emotional needs.

If you have parents or in-laws staying close by, that could work well too. In my case, we had an arrangement where-in the in-laws or parents would come and stay with us alternately. When my first son was born, we continued with this arrangement for the initial few years. Till the time my mother retired, and they could move to the same city as us. Having parents around was a blessing while my two boys grew up. Not only was their physical well-being taken care of, but also value-based grooming.

We always had a nanny to support while the kids were still small. She could do all the stuff around the childcare. The supervision of my parents allowed me to be mentally at peace while I was at work. I luckily did not have to manage remotely the activities of the maids at home. This allowed me to put complete focus on work while I was in the office. Apart from a stray call if there was an emergency or a quick input was needed, I was most times left undisturbed during the working hours.

To put your professional foot forward, it is imperative to have an unwavering backup system at home. For example, if you are solely dependent on maids, you would need to account for days when they take unplanned leave or quit suddenly. However, since I had parents around, they could support essential activities like feeding the kids.

What happens if the maid calls in sick? Will that impact your workday? Will you need to take leave, or is there any other way to manage? Or are you having a dependable daycare centre nearby?

I have seen that a good daycare centre could work as well. If you have one close to your house or workplace, that could work. Having it close to the workplace provides the added advantage to drop in during the lunch break. Some of the companies I know have started providing daycare facilities for the kids of their employees. It depends on the facility and how professionally it is being run.

Whatever may be your choice, it may be a good idea to first experiment with one hour of having your kid experience it. You may even wish to sit in for the initial few minutes to see whether it would work out in the long run.

Another thing to figure out is how do you manage if your kid falls sick. What are the policies that the daycare has for kids who are not feeling well?

Do they have a sick bay or an isolation room? Do they have a call-in doctor facility or a nurse on call? These are all questions to explore.

Also, as a family, you may wish to discuss with your spouse how you would manage such emergencies. For example, do you have a work-from-home option? Will you be able to take leave? Is your workplace ok with such kind of emergency leave?

Not all questions can be answered in advance. You may need to take a decision based on the situation on that particular day. For example, do you have an important deliverable on that day? Does your partner need to make an important presentation that cannot be skipped? Whose organization is more supportive of child-care leave? What is helpful is having a broad understanding of taking shared responsibility for finding solutions.

Incidentally, the idea that our parents come to pitch in for our kids' upbringing was proposed by my husband. At the onset, though, we did not know if it would work. It started more like a trial thing. Though soon, we could find a rhythm of what could work out. There were times when the parents had some priorities to take care of. Those were times when we both pitched in and made it work. Of course, it was an exception, and the supervisors were gracious enough to understand and allow leave at such times.

Was it the best arrangement? At that time, it was not easy to plan travel and tickets and manage all logistics. Both parents had their different ways of managing the kids and the household. Adjusting during transitions was an uphill task for all. What we learnt was that kids have a fantastic ability to adapt. They could understand the elders and adapt quickly to the change.

And I feel they got the best of both worlds. With a diverse set of values, they were able to imbibe the important beliefs of both families.

And we could tide over some of the growing years of the kids while continuing the career journey. Each family has its unique strengths, and you need to figure out what would work out best for you and the family. Your ability to organize will also determine how you can take on more passion projects, as covered in the next chapter.

## **ASK YOURSELF:**

For you to be able to focus on work, you need to organize your home well. If you have kids, the child-care arrangements will be essential. Some of the things to figure out.

- Is your home well-organized for someone to manage when you are travelling?
- Do you regularly de-clutter and organize the essential spaces like the kitchen?
- What are the child-care arrangements that you would like to opt for?
- Do you have a backup in case the nanny for the baby calls in sick?
- Can parents or in-laws support, or do you have supportive neighbours?

## ORGANISE LIFE

| Core | Reflect |
|---|---|
| Organise the house and everything within it well.<br><br>Have a place for everything and everything should have a place.<br><br>Declutter and stream-line processes regularly.<br><br>Have an unwavering backup system at home | How easy would it be to find things in your house?<br><br>Frequency and periodicity of de-cluttering<br><br>People who can accept the hand-me-downs<br><br>Can your house run if you or your spouse are out?<br><br>How strong is your support network? |

| Key Practices | |
|---|---|
| Labelling and sorting out space and shelves can be a great idea.<br><br>Declutter monthly or quarterly and identify the go-to people to give away stuff.<br><br>Strengthen processes to make them less dependent on people. | Invest in people, trust them and let them do their work! While you do magic in your workspace.<br><br>Discuss with your near and dear ones, how you would manage emergencies. Finally take decision based on the situation on that particular day |

| Explore | Potential Journeys |
|---|---|
| Can anyone else step in to manage your house while you are away?<br><br>Working out your spaces to ensure that anyone at one glance can find things.<br><br>Is one support able to substitute for another? | Declutter to Feel Good - Ana Ericsson<br><br>5s Home - Ade Asefeso<br><br>Developing and putting back-ups in place<br><br>Building support ecosystem and relationships<br><br>Maintaining consistency in support team |

# Chapter 9: Passion Projects

What are some of the things that you are passionate about? What are the things that you could do at 2 am if someone woke you from sleep?

When we are passionate about something, we do not wait for someone else to tell us to do it. Instead, we are internally motivated to do it and achieve more. Neither do we wait for someone to reward us for what we have done. Instead, the work itself becomes the reward.

There are multiple books around the topic of finding your Ikigai. This concept is also linked to longevity. If we can find the intersection where our passion meets the world's needs, we can make that our profession.

***Choose a job you love, and you will never have to work a day in your life.***

- **Confucius**

From the time we were in school, we have been asked a question. What is your favourite subject? Most often, this subject was the one we scored highest in. Or the teacher was phenomenal. Or we just had a strong inclination to read more of this subject. It just came easily to us. Most often, our decision to pursue this subject depended on this initial inclination.

As we grow up, we sometimes let go of this internal liking compass. Instead, we start chasing goals in the outer world. We look at high-paying jobs. Or jobs that can take us abroad or look for organisations that can give us better packages and perks.

In this exercise, we forget to consult our hearts. What are the things that our heart beats for? What is it that you strongly believe in? What is that one dream that you want to fulfil?

Once we start knowing more about what we like, we can find more of those opportunities outside. But, on the other hand, if we start looking for jobs outside first, it is like putting the cart in front of the horse!

Then we spend a lifetime dragging ourselves to work.

> Miriam was interested in fashion and make-up. She wanted to pursue this line of profession and become a professional - make-up artist. It was not considered such a viable option by her family, though. She ended up pursuing a career in Finance. Crunching numbers through the day was not something she liked.
>
> But given that her income did help the family, she continued in the field. She was

not satisfied with how things were shaping up on her career front. She then decided to pursue a weekend course in beauty and make-up. Soon enough, she was able to help her friends with their beauty needs. Miriam decided to take a sabbatical and work with this idea. Soon she was getting orders for make-up for all video shoots within her social circle. Once she saw that this could be an option she could earn from, she quit her job. Seven years on, she loves the work she does. The flexibility and being her own boss, have been additional perks, that she is very happy about.

Even while in a job, it is always a good idea to keep looking for dream projects; something that makes your heart go boom; work that engages your heart, mind, and soul and something that gets you into the 'flow'.

That is when you lose the sense of time. You forget yourself and your surroundings. The only thing you are focused on is that piece of work. Minutes turn to hours, and you are glued to creating your masterpiece. You remember neither hunger nor thirst. All your senses are focused only on one area.

This flow not just creates good work. It boosts your creativity. It brings you into the present moment, and you are only aware of the 'here and now'. You lose the sense of the external environment, and the other people stop mattering. All that matters is that you are working on your most passionate work.

This also improves your overall well-being. Your satisfaction levels improve. You concentrate better. The chemicals released in your brain; help you reach a better state. In this state, you feel mentally and physically much better.

When you are working on this project, you find such joy that the process itself becomes a pleasure. You no longer need any external motivation. The rewards and recognition just become a by-product of your stellar performance. What you can achieve is phenomenal. People around can see your brilliance, and appreciation just comes naturally.

Finding these passion projects can be a great way to improve your performance at work. And it does help to improve your overall well-being. It works as an energizer, providing energy to concentrate on other things that you need to do.

So how do you get selected for these prime projects? It is simple; you need to negotiate for being considered for projects and special initiatives. Putting your hand up and keeping it up may require patience and perseverance. If you are a married woman with kids, people may assume that you will not be interested in any other additional responsibilities. The fact that you are interested may become a surprise to most. In that case, highlighting your interest may be worthwhile. Not just once, but again and again. You may need to share this not just with your direct supervisor but also with other function heads.

Then when you get asked, you need to sign up and seal the deal quickly. You may have fears cropping up in an instant. Will I be able to manage? How will I find time for this along with my other responsibilities? How will my kids and husband manage? Will I be able to have a work-life balance?

Impostor syndrome is something that can easily paralyze us. Where we think, 'Am I good enough to do this'? Do not let the fears manage you. Instead, you need to tell yourself that 'I can do it' actively. Sure, there will be a stretch. But then no growth happens in the comfort zone!

So, you will need to go through the growing pains to allow your professional success to expand. You may need to keep negotiating your way from one project to the next. But, you will notice that once you show your interest and dedication in one, you soon get counted in the list of probable resources for next.

> Shehnaz was a go-getter from the time she joined the organisation. She liked her work and was happy to put in long hours. As she completed two years, she could see that she had mastered her current role. It took her less time to complete the activities, and

now the tasks seemed much more manageable. However, she wondered what she could do further to help her development. In the performance discussion, she asked her supervisor for advice. Though the manager did not have an immediate answer, he said he would come back.

In the meantime, Shehnaz started taking small initiatives in her area. Thinking about how small projects could help streamline work and make it more efficient. Seeing her passion and energy, the manager nominated her for one of the company's projects. This was a great learning opportunity for Shehnaz. Moreover, it was in one of the areas that she liked, which was just the cherry on the cake!

Once you have the passion projects lined up there is one more final step to add to completion. Last but not the least, it is all about loving and accepting yourself as shared in the next chapter.

## **ASK YOURSELF:**

Following your passion is one of the greatest delights. Yet, not all of us may know for sure what is that area. If we are aware, we may find it challenging to find work in that area. The idea is to start small:

- Are you aware of the areas that you are genuinely passionate about?
- Is this area something that the world needs and can create value for others?
- Does your current role have some of these elements included already that you can expand?
- Is your organisation currently having any opportunities that could leverage your passion and strengths?
- Do you wish to start a hobby project around this area to experience flow?

# PASSION PROJECTS

| Core | Reflect |
|---|---|
| When we are passionate about something, we are internally motivated to do it and achieve really phenomenal. The work itself becomes the reward and significantly impacts the quality and longevity of life. | Growth happens outside the comfort zone.<br><br>Are you letting go of internal liking compass?<br><br>Is work becoming a drag or an easy flow?<br><br>Do you let the fears manage your life?<br><br>How is work contributing to overall wellbeing? |

| Key Practices | |
|---|---|
| Even while in a job, it is always a good idea to keep looking for passion projects.<br><br>Negotiate for being considered for projects and special initiatives. Putting your hand up and keep it up with patience and perseverance. | Highlighting genuine interest may be worthwhile. Not just once, but again and again to all relevant stakeholders<br><br>When you get asked for contributing in a passion project, quickly sign up and seal the deal. Don't worry about the potential 'stretch' |

| Explore | Potential Journeys |
|---|---|
| Finding Ikigai | Ikigai - Hector Garcia, Francesc Miralles |
| Work that engages your heart, mind and soul | Finding Flow – Mihaly Csikszentmihalyi |
| One dream that you dearly want to come true | Pursuing interests seriously and consistently |
| Something that gets you in 'flow' | Starting small with passion projects |
| When you lose the sense of time and all your senses are focused only in one area | Following and believing internal liking compass |

# Chapter 10: Loving Yourself

Some questions to start self-exploration can be, 'Do you love yourself? Why is it important for you? Does it matter? You love or hate yourself – is it of any relevance?'

There may be different answers that may come up for you. My take on it - it is important.

The world is like a mirror. It reflects what we think and feel. If you love yourself, the chances are that love will get reflected. You will get the appreciation and accolades you deserve.

If you do not appreciate yourself, then an excellent place to start working on is your self-worth. Your outward worldly success is hugely dependent on your inner worth.

If feelings of self-doubt bother you a lot, then you may need to fix that. One way of doing that is through affirmations. I have been a big fan of Louise Hay. In her book, 'You can Heal your Life', she talks about some of these affirmations that can be used.

The art is to keep these in the present. In this way, you can trick your subconscious mind into believing the affirmation to be true. For example, you could say the dialogue to yourself looking in the mirror or writing it down.

Tell yourself often – "I love you". The other affirmations that I have tried are, 'I am strong', 'I am powerful', 'I am healthy', 'I am a money magnet', 'I attract abundance'.

When we cannot accept ourselves, how can we expect others to love and adore us? With affirmations, self-love starts permeating all aspects of your life. Personally, it helps your relationships grow stronger. This is because you trust and accept others as they are. Rather than changing your spouse into an ideal spouse, you learn to live with the flaws. Professionally, it allows you to grow by breaking some of your limiting beliefs.

Another interesting way is to try 'gratitude'. For example, you could try to say out loud, Thank you, Universe, for giving me an understanding and loving life partner'. 'Thank you for the wonderful kids that I have.' 'Thank you for the supportive and caring family.' 'Thank you for giving me a job I love' and so on.

Self-healing is another close step to self-love.

Often when I would fall sick, I would go through the list of diseases that the book 'You can Heal your life' has at the end.

Looking at my thought patterns, I could discover where am I stuck. Repeating the new thought patterns did bring relief. I am not saying that we do not need medication when prescribed. It is more like trying to supplement it with a thought process to support the healing process. Then you get the healing process to happen faster and better.

Any disease is the way the body is giving us feedback on the 'unease'. It is up to us to read the message and take action. Just taking some time off to reflect can be a starting point. When we get too busy, we take the body for granted. We refuse to notice the initial signals. That is when there could be a break-down, and you end up taking sick time-off.

> Shivani was an accountant in a small firm. She had been working in this area for more than ten years. She was always in hurry and trying to multi-task to manage her work most efficiently. She did have lots of falls and accidents as a result. Mostly minor, but some that lead to fractures. She wondered, 'what is the problem?' Till she met someone who told her to work on her mental patterns. Once she started doing that, the accidents started disappearing almost magically.

Self-healing has been something that I have been learning about. Pranic healing was again something that I was intrigued by. I had taken an introductory course in pranic healing that covered the fundamentals and some techniques. One of the most straightforward techniques that I have tried is taking a salt bath—using salt as an agent for cleansing myself of diseased energy.

Meditation was something that I got introduced to when I turned 18. It has been something that has stuck to me. However, I am always trying to get more regular with it. This is something that I have learned to depend on during my most trying times. Strangely it almost feels like the antidote for all problems—mental, as well as physical. But, then, I believe that most physical ailments are the impact of mental stress and strain. If we can fix the thought pattern, the disease may disappear as well.

What is your spiritual anchor? The technique that you use is not the significant bit. The fact that you have multiple go-to choices is what is more important.

When the pandemic stuck in 2020, we were scampering around, looking at options to give us some mental respite from the anxiety and fear. At such times, what works is having some tricks up your sleeves to self-soothe.

Another interesting concept that I discovered was energy healing. I have been following the videos of Donna Eden. We all are, at the end of the day energy – driven. You would find days when you feel drained, as if the body battery is on empty. These could be typical days when you have had fewer engaging tasks or conversations. Maybe you had to spend the time firefighting, focusing on crisis management.

Nevertheless, there are days when you are doing work that you are passionate about. You are focusing on the tasks that you love doing. You are operating from your strength areas and adding tremendous value to others around you. This leaves you accomplishing much more in a single day than you would in a week. Though you have been working non-stop, end of the day, you feel more energized. There is a skip in your step and a smile on your face.

***If we learn to manage our energy, we can achieve a lot more.***

Donna talks about simple tapping techniques that you can apply easily. For example, when the work-from-home era started, I started feeling an energy drop in the afternoon. As the work was there to finish as per timelines, I began to practise five-minute energizing routine. Just by tapping at a few points, I could sense a change in my energy levels. I also started exploring other energy routines, like the one that can be used if you feel a sense of overwhelm.

What do you believe in? Do you find all these things mumbo-jumbo? It does not matter if you believe in these same techniques. Do what works for you. Do what you believe. Then you will see magic manifesting for you.

There is a book by Dr Wayne Dyer, 'You will see it when you believe it'. I think that is so true for each and everything in our lives. The first step is that we start believing in our self, our power. Once we do that, we can then go on to achieve anything.

These were some things at the energy level. Then there are things at the physical level. Life is all about maintaining the balance between the two.

So how do you show love to yourself at the physical level – by taking care of your body.

Eat well to start with. We all know in theory what is good, nutritious, wholesome food. Fads apart, those keep changing. Having a balanced diet is essential. I have an elder sister who used to have a very determined inclination to eat healthy food right from the start. So, given that siblings always need to compete, I would try to eat what she was having. This was primarily fruit, milkshakes, protein-rich food. It meant more protein, vitamins, minerals, and less junk.

From an early time, I would pick healthy food options and modulate my food habits around them. I am happy that I am blessed with a naturally high rate of metabolism. So that took care of burning the calories quickly as well.

For every person, it is crucial to understand your system. The diet needs to be aligned with how your body responds to certain foods. For example, when do you feel naturally the hungriest in a day? Are there food items that make you feel bloated? Are there fruits that you love to eat in a season?

> Let us talk about Anjana. She was an air hostess, and the work required her to travel almost 15 to 20 days each month, taking her across time zones and different geographies. When she returned home, she was too tired to cook. Since her sleep cycle was disturbed, she found it difficult to fall back into a routine after the travel. The result was a high dependence on fast food, mostly picked up from roadside vendors. Erratic sleeping also did not allow any time for exercise.

Nevertheless, she liked the high-flying lifestyle, and the perks were incredible. Then suddenly, one day, she experienced abdominal pain and had to be rushed to the doctor. The doctor gave her a clear warning to change her lifestyle or prepare for more suffering. The continuous eating out had taken a toll on her stomach lining that was showing irritation. So Anjana took a few days off and then started getting into a better life rhythm.

I have tried to stick to my food intuition. I am hungriest in the morning. Any heavy, calorie-rich food I can digest in the morning. As the sun goes down, so does my appetite for fatty, spicy food. I am not too much of a fan of chillies, and I'm fine having bland food. I love eating seasonal fruits like mango, litchi, cherries. Yet, my -all-year-round staple is banana. I love this fruit for its simplicity and easy availability. Also, it can give you a boost of energy when you need it most. I do have a sweet tooth. But I try to keep it in balance by having sweets between meals rather than after meals.

The focus needs to be on having balanced meals with all colours of vegetables and fruits. The other part is to include a good mix of proteins and carbohydrates.

Also, keeping a bottle of water handy is a must. I have always stepped out of the house with a bottle of water. If you can have at least 3-4 litres of water throughout the day, it is excellent.

Doing regular exercise is the next form of self-care. The more you keep your body moving, the more you will remain agile. It is simple here as well, use it or lose it. As kids, we can do all sorts of acrobatics easily. But, as we get into a more sedentary life, the movements get restricted. Then we realise that aches and pains are slowly replacing the flexibility of the body. Trying to overcome pain through physiotherapy then becomes essential. But the recovery process is slow. Coming back to the earlier levels get more challenging. So, a better way is to go for prevention rather than cure.

Walking is one of the best forms of exercise. It is simple and does not require any equipment or inherent cost. Whatever your lifestyle or work may be, incorporating a 30-minute walk may not be such an uphill task. But, then, where there is a will, there is a way!

Amelia was working as a sales manager in a multinational company. Her work required her to sit for long hours during the day. On other days she would need to be travelling across the country to meet clients. At times the journey started early morning, and she returned late at night. This was taking a toll on her back, and she had chronic back pain. She sometimes took a pain killer and went for a few physiotherapy sessions. Then, one day as she was stepping out for work, she felt a snap in the back. It was a sharp pain that left her unable to move. She was rushed to the hospital, where it was diagnosed as a muscle spasm. She was advised bed rest for a few days as the MRI showed some changes as well. Once recovered, Amelia took to yoga with zeal. This one incident made her realise that she was taking her back for granted. With regular back exercises, her pain reduced.

Exercise in any form you like. The important thing is to have some form of physical activity during the day! Yoga, dance, Zumba, aerobics are all great ways to keep moving. The exercise also releases endorphins that keep you mentally happy and charged. Physical training also takes away your attention from day-to-day problems. It gets your mind in the present. So, make it a priority and find a way to get moving at least four days a week.

Sleep is the next thing that can help you recharge and augment your performance. With social media exposure, we all cut down on sleep hours. It is important to sleep 7-8 hours to feel fresh the following day. Our ability to focus, creativity, empathy are all impacted adversely if we are tired and groggy. Have a set time for bed and try relaxation techniques to fall off to sleep. You can wake up at a fixed time each day and plan a morning routine to help you set the right tone for the day.

One way to start the day could be – to pray. We often underestimate the power of prayer until we hit a roadblock. Prayer is not an alternative to doing what we have to do. It is more like a complementary force that helps us achieve what we set out to do. It helps us to align ourselves internally and have self-belief. It provides us with the trust that there is a superpower that is supporting us in the universe. This faith helps us to move mountains.

You need to ask yourself – Do I believe in the existence of any superpower? The name is not important here. Are you a spiritual person? Are you a religious person? Are you an atheist? Do you believe in 'karma' in terms of 'you reap, what you sow'? Do you believe that work is worship?

Our beliefs are often shaped as per our family or environment. There is no need to change them drastically until you feel the need to do so. What is essential is to check. Are those beliefs still serving you? If yes, then you can go ahead with the same set of beliefs. If not, then you need to evaluate and update them.

The external reality keeps changing with time. But sometimes, our inner world of beliefs is the same as what the little boy or girl at the age of 7 years would have believed. If you find some ideologies that may no longer be relevant, it will be good to change them. It is not required to start changing everything all at once. It will be good to make small changes.

The same is with faith. Praying in front of an idol is not the only way. Meditation, chanting, or any other thing that works for you. Even journaling can be a therapeutic exercise. You may choose any one or many ways to connect. It is all about finding ways to connect your power with the super-power in the universe.

When you are in trouble, you would then feel sufficiently anchored and supported. When you have good times, you can be grateful and say a prayer of gratitude. Whatever we focus on expands. When we find ourselves having an abundance, we can continue to count our blessings. This sends a simple message to the universe to expand that abundance further.

Prayers have a lot of power. Whenever I feel stuck, I write a small prayer in my journal and sit with my eyes closed at the end of the day. It does, for me, take away the mental worry and then I go about doing what I need to do with better focus.

The universe is here to support us. Then why not leverage its power?

## **ASK YOURSELF:**

- Do you have a daily self-care routine for yourself?
- How do you ensure a balanced diet and a healthy lifestyle?
- Do you have some form of exercise included in your day?
- How many hours of sleep are you able to clock in every night?
- Do you use techniques like meditation or prayer for mental rejuvenation?

## LOVING YOURSELF

| Core | Reflect |
|---|---|
| Love yourself and the universe will shower love on you.<br><br>You will get all the appreciation and accolades in the journey of becoming your biggest fan.<br><br>Embrace your imperfections to expedite your progress. | What is essential is to check our beliefs. Are they still serving us or coming in the way?<br><br>If some ideologies and beliefs are no longer relevant, then it will be good to make small shifts regularly.<br><br>Unlearn and let go. |

| Key Practices | |
|---|---|
| Believing in our own self, our own power is the starting point. Once we are able to do that, we can then go on to achieve anything.<br><br>Practice loving yourself at physical level – by eating right, sticking to own food intuition, staying hydrated and exercising consistently | Adequate sleep with fixed sleep hours and energising morning routine can help us recharge and augment our performance.<br><br>Prayers are complementary force that helps us achieve what we set out to do. Praying keep our faith steadfast which can make us move mountains. |

| Explore | Potential Journeys |
|---|---|
| Having self-doubt, try affirmations | You Can Heal Your Life - Louis Hay |
| Feeling inadequate, explore gratitude | Energy Healing - Donna Eden |
| Getting restless, give meditation a chance | You will see it, When you believe it - Wayne Dyer Pranic Healing |
| Stressed too often, develop a spiritual anchor | Meditation |
| Self-heal the way that works best for you | |

# Chapter 11: The final word

To conclude, we all have unique experiences as we move through life. Yet, though the circumstances and context differ, some common threads run across. What is needed is to keep observing those around us and learning from their experiences too. Books are one way of learning from the documented learning of others.

Life is too short for making all the mistakes and then learning from them. That is why we can strive to live our life to the fullest and yet keep viewing the success of others. Sometimes our view of ourselves influences our decisions.

Are we women first? Is gender the critical differentiator? How do you define yourself? As a woman? As a mother? As a wife? Or is your qualification and competence a more significant part of your personality? Is being a professional core to your being?

As we draw more power from our performance and influence, gender does not matter as much. We have our unique way of working and relating as women, but that does not need to become a handicap. Empathy, care, and intuition will be the key skills for the post-covid world. With the feminine energy at the core, can we lead and grow?

We have to balance it well with the entrepreneurial spirit and risk-taking ability. Success is a journey towards excellence and meaning. We are happiest when we achieve our targets, and we are in sync with our life goals. Although we may operate from any of our strengths, the critical piece is to find the best solution given the situation and constraints.

Our grooming may have been done in a particular way, but, today we have the intelligence and wisdom to learn and channelize our energy in any direction that we choose.

Connecting with others in the most authentic way and sharing who we are is a key to forming deep relations. So keep talking to family and friends to honour the supportive relationships around you strong.

Learning each day something new to empower yourself is essential. This can be just a book, or it could be the inspiration to start a life-long journey to win!

There have been many people who had provided inspiration and support when I needed it most. Professionally and personally, there have been many who were there when I felt lost. I have a lot of appreciation and gratitude for all these individuals who made my journey possible.

For me, there is a lot to achieve and to conquer ahead. Therefore, I look forward to the next happening decade in my life.

I hope this book works like a lucky charm for all the readers.

# **Bibliography**

- Who Moved My Cheese? – book by Dr. Spencer Johnson.
- You Can Heal Your Life - book by Louise Hay.
- Flow: The Psychology of Optimal Experience – book by Mihaly Csikszentmihalyi.
- Energy Medicine – book by Donna Eden.
- You'll See it when you believe it – book by Dr. Wayne Dyer.
- Ikigai: The Japanese secret to a long and happy life – book by Héctor García and Francesc Miralles.
- Lean In – book by Sheryl Sanderg.
- Survival of the Savvy – book by Rick Brandon and Marty Seldman.
- The Power of Vulnerability – TED talk by Brené Brown.
- The Power of believing that you can improve – TED talk by Carol Dweck

# Acknowledgements

I would like to thank all the people who have supported me in the journey of writing this book and in my life till now.

I start by thanking my parents for bringing me up to believe I could achieve the highest goals possible. Also, my sister who led the path of studying and working hard and becoming the perfect role model. To my extended family for providing me inspiration and leading by example always.

My husband for supporting unconditionally in my career and at home with the kids and everything else. As I got involved in strengthening my career and creating this book, I have leaned on him more and more. He has been my pillar of strength when I needed most. My father-in-law and mother-in-law for supporting me through my journey of motherhood and encouraging me to manage both my career and home. My brother-in-law for being a great sounding board at all challenging times and my sister-in-law for being like a caring friend.

My two boys who continue to delight me with everything that they do. By managing most of their school-work independently, they have given me the courage to go chase my own goals.

Many of my colleagues who are now friends, work-life would not have been same without you.

My friends who have stayed by my side as I became the person I am today. To all those who have mentored and coached me at crucial career stages, whenever I felt stuck.

I would like to thank Geeta Sahai, the editor for this book, for helping me bring this book in its current shape and form. And, last but not the least, Som Bathla for making this book a reality.

The journey of life has been filled with learning and this book has helped me crystallize some of that.

# About The Author

Anshu Bhargava is a Human Resources professional with 15 years of solid corporate experience behind her. She has worked in companies like TCS, Owens Corning, DNV. She has travelled to places like Dubai, Singapore, Australia, Amsterdam, Canada as part of work-related and personal pursuits.

Born and brought up in Delhi. She currently stays in Mumbai, India with her spouse and two boys.

She is a Masters in Human Resources from International Management Institute. Bachelor of Information Technology from Delhi University. With a passion for helping people live their dreams, she has been coaching leaders. From the early days of her career, she has been a trainer and facilitator. Her areas of expertise span across communication, leadership, resilience, collaboration, growth mindset

In the last few years, she has been working in the area of diversity & inclusion. She feels strongly about gender diversity in organisations. Given the skew in the number of women in leadership roles, she feels a deep sense of urgency to help women progress in their journey as they climb the corporate ladder. This book is an attempt to weave in her experiences and learnings. Few of these her own and others from the women who have been alongside, in the vicinity, trail-blazing their path.

With this book, she attempts to give a gentle nudge to all women who are feeling stuck and stagnant in their careers. Wondering where they are failing and looking for that supportive guidance to create their breakthrough. Though this is an offering of love for all women, the principles are pretty much universal.

www.ingramcontent.com/pod-product-compliance
Lightning Source LLC
Chambersburg PA
CBHW070655220526
45466CB00001B/450